DEC 2 9 2011

D1552091

Animal Life Cycles

# Penguin

by Wendy Perkins

amicus readers
2

**amicus readers**

# Say hello to amicus readers.

You'll find our helpful dog, Amicus, chasing a ball—to let you know the reading level of a book.

## A

### Learn to Read

Frequent repetition of sentence structures, high frequency words, and familiar topics provide ample support for brand new readers. Approximately 100 words.

## 1

### Read Independently

Repetition is mixed with varied sentence structures and 6 to 8 content words per book are introduced with photo label and picture glossary supports. Approximately 150 words.

## 2

### Read to Know More

These books feature a higher text load with additional nonfiction features such as more photos, time lines, and text divided into sections. Approximately 250 words.

Amicus Readers are published by Amicus
P.O. Box 1329, Mankato, Minnesota 56002

U.S. publication copyright © 2012 Amicus.
International copyright reserved in all countries.
No part of this book may be reproduced in any
form without written permission from the publisher.

Series Editor          Rebecca Glaser
Series Designer        Heather Dreisbach
Photo Researcher       Heather Dreisbach

Printed in the United States of America at
Corporate Graphics in North Mankato, Minnesota.

1023
3-2011

10 9 8 7 6 5 4 3 2 1

Library of Congress Cataloging-in-Publication Data
Perkins, Wendy, 1957-
    Penguin / by Wendy Perkins.
        p. cm. – (Amiucs Readers. Animal life cycles)
    Includes index.
    Summary: "Presents the life cycle of a penguin from
    mating and laying eggs to adult. Includes time line
    of life cycle and sequencing activity"–Provided by
    publisher.
    ISBN 978-1-60753-158-6 (library binding)
    1. Penguins–Life cycles–Juvenile literature. I. Title.
    QL696.S473P457 2012
    598.4'4–dc22
                                        2010035669

# Table of Contents

# A Life Cycle

Swoosh! A penguin rides a wave onto the beach. It stands up and waddles toward a group of penguins called a colony.  A penguin's life cycle begins in a breeding colony.

breeding

egg

adult

chick

5

# Breeding

The male penguin calls to attract a female. Some penguins also move their heads and wings in a kind of dance. If a female likes the male's calls and dance, they will breed.

# Egg

The female lays one or two eggs. She and her mate take turns keeping them warm and safe. After about one month, the eggs hatch. The male and female take turns staying with the chicks. The other parent feeds in the ocean.

hatching

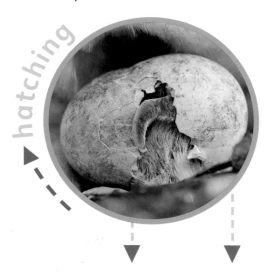

Breeding —— Laying eggs —— Eggs hatch 1 month later

rock nest

egg

# Chick

When the chicks are two to three weeks old, both parents go off to feed during the day. To stay safe, penguin chicks huddle together in a big group called a crèche (KRESH).

Breeding — Laying eggs — Eggs hatch 1 month later — Chicks stay in crèche 2–3 weeks old —

The parents eat many fish. Later, they spit some up for their young. A chick sticks its head inside the adult's mouth to get the food.

Breeding — Laying eggs — Eggs hatch 1 month later — Chicks stay in crèche 2–3 weeks old —

Fluffy feathers called down keep the chicks warm. After seven weeks, short, stiff feathers appear. The young penguins enter the water and learn to swim.

Breeding — Laying eggs — Eggs hatch 1 month later — Chicks stay in crèche 2–3 weeks old —

Chicks grow
feathers
7 weeks old

Once they can swim well, the young penguins begin to chase and catch fish. At five months old, they can feed themselves.

Breeding — Laying eggs — Eggs hatch 1 month later — Chicks stay in crèche 2–3 weeks old —

Chicks grow
feathers
7 weeks old

Young penguins
feed themselves
5 months old

## Adult

Penguins can live for about twenty years. They begin breeding when they are about five years old. Males call and dance. Females choose a mate. The penguin life cycle continues.

Breeding — Laying eggs — Eggs hatch 1 month later — Chicks stay in crèche 2–3 weeks old

Chicks grow
feathers
7 weeks old

Young penguins
feed themselves
5 months old

Adult penguins
begin breeding
5 years old

# Photo Glossary

**breed**
to find a mate and produce young; male penguins dance to attract a mate

**chick**
a baby penguin

**colony**
a group of penguins that breeds and raises chicks together

**crèche**
a group of young animals that gather together for safety while their parents are away

## down

soft, fluffy feathers that keep a bird warm; penguin chicks are born with down

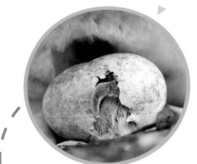

## hatch

to break out of an egg

## life cycle

the stages of an animal's life from birth to death

## mate

a male and female animal that breed together

# Life Cycle Puzzle

The stages of a penguin's life are all mixed up.
Can you put them in the right order?

grow feathers

egg

breeding

chick

adult

catch fish

# Ideas for Parents and Teachers

Children are fascinated by animals, and even more so by life cycles as they grow up themselves. *Animal Life Cycles*, an Amicus Readers Level 2 series, lets kids compare life stages of animals. The books use labels and a photo glossary to introduce new vocabulary. The activity page and time lines reinforce sequencing skills.

### Before Reading

- Read the title and ask the children to tell what they know about babies or baby animals.
- Have the students talk about whether they've seen penguins before.
- Look at the photo glossary words. Tell children to watch for them as they read the book.

### Read the Book

- "Walk" through the book and look at the photos. Point out the time line showing how long penguins spend at each stage.
- Ask the students to read the book independently.
- Provide support where necessary. Show students how the highlighted words are explained in the photo glossary.

### After Reading

- Have students do the activity on page 22 and put the stages of the penguin life cycle in order.
- Compare the life cycle of a penguin with other animals in the series. Does it have the same number of stages?
- Have the students compare the human life cycle to a penguin's life cycle. How is it different? How is it the same?

# Index

# Web Sites

**Adelie Penguin—National Geographic Kids**
http://kids.nationalgeographic.com/Animals/CreatureFeature,
Adelie-penguin

**KidZone Penguins**
http://www.kidzone.ws/animals/penguins/index.htm

**Kids' Corner—Penguin Planet**
http://kevinschafer.com/penguinplanet/kids.html